IS IT HEAVY OR LIGHT?

by Sheila Rivera

first step nonfiction

Lerner Publications Company · Minneapolis

This brick is heavy.

This feather is light.

This pumpkin is heavy.

This glass is light.

This box is heavy.

This egg is light.

Are you heavy or light?